Everything You Need to Know

WHEN A
PARENT
HAS AIDS

It's never easy for a person with AIDS to tell family members about his or her illness.

Everything You Need to Know
WHEN A
PARENT
HAS AIDS

Barbara Hermie Draimin

THE ROSEN PUBLISHING GROUP, INC.
NEW YORK

Published in 1994 by The Rosen Publishing Group, Inc.
29 East 21st Street, New York, NY 10010

First Edition
Copyright 1994 by The Rosen Publishing Group, Inc.

Manufactured in the United States of America.

Library of Congress Cataloging-in-Publication Data

Draimin, Barbara Hermie.
    Everything you need to know when a parent has AIDS / Barbara
Hermie Draimin. — 1st ed.
        p.   cm. (The Need to know library)
    Includes bibliographical references and index.
    ISBN 0-8239-1690-1
    1. AIDS (Disease)—Juvenile literature. 2. Children of AIDS
patients—Juvenile literature. [1. AIDS (Disease) 2. Parent and child.
3. Sick—Family relationships. 4. Diseases.] I. Title. II. Series.
RC607.A26D732 1994
616.97'92—dc20   94-15969
                                                                        CIP
                                                                         AC

Contents

1. Karen and John   7

2. Does My Parent Have AIDS?   11

3. Facts about HIV and AIDS   16

4. Will I Get AIDS?   23

5. Preventing HIV   27

6. What AIDS Does to a Family   33

7. Whom Can I Tell?   39

8. What Illness and Death Look Like   45

9. Starting Again   53

    Glossary—*Explaining New Words*   58

    Help List   60

    For Further Reading   62

    Index   63

Attending support-group meetings can be helpful for family members living with a person with AIDS.

Chapter 1

Karen and John

Karen walked into the classroom for the first time. She was there to attend a meeting for kids who had relatives who had died. Five teens were standing together talking. Karen didn't know anyone and wanted to disappear. The social worker asked her to come and sit beside her. She said that everyone was nervous the first time.

Karen looked at the other students. They looked regular to her. There were three boys and two girls. They could have been in the cafeteria talking about anything. But she knew that each one was like her in a particular way: Each had lost a sister, brother, father, or mother in the last year.

John left the group and came over to Karen. "Hi, I'm John. I know what it's like your first time.

This is my third time, and it does get easier. We'll all help you; you'll see. You don't have to hide your secrets here. We all have them. Yours probably aren't even the worst."

The social worker asked everyone to sit down so that the meeting could start.

"This is Karen. It's her first day, and she's just going to listen to see what goes on here. Who would like to start?"

A boy said, "My dad and I went out to the cemetery this weekend, and it was awful. I hate that place. I don't know why he always wants to go. It is so depressing—all those stones. That's not how I remember my mother. She was the busiest person I knew until the day of the car accident. She has been gone for four months, and I still come downstairs in the morning thinking that she will be there with breakfast. Sometimes I even think I see her at the mall when someone who looks like her walks by. I don't think I'll ever get used to it."

John said, "My mom had cancer for three years. I feel bad that by the end I was hoping she would die. I even imagined what her funeral would be like. She lost sixty pounds and was all bony. She was so tired that she couldn't lift her head. It was awful. My whole life was about her illness. Every time we made plans, Mom would get sick. Going to the hospital was so hard. When she came home from the hospital, it was hard, too. In fact, it was all hard. For some crazy reason, Dad didn't want me to tell people about her being sick. He said it was our family's business and no one else's. I was always making up stories about where I was going and what I was doing. My younger brother, who is three years old, has no idea what happened. He asks me if Mom has come back from the store yet. Sometimes I think I'm living in the twilight zone. At least when I come here I can tell the truth."

Karen learned that the group met once a week, and students were excused from classes to attend. The social worker called it "family group," but everyone in the school knew what it was really about. Karen was glad to have a place to come and hear the real thing. She wondered most why people are so hush-hush about illness and death.

At the end of the meeting Karen said, "Why are grown-ups always whispering and telling kids to tell white lies when someone is sick? If everybody dies at some point, why is death such a mystery? My relatives act as if we had done something wrong. I mean, it's not as if I killed my father. He got sick and he died. This is all a puzzle to me."

No one in the group tried to answer Karen. But everyone had the same kind of story to tell. Each person felt a little guilty and didn't know why. Each person felt sad and wasn't allowed to show those feelings in public. It seemed that the whole family changed when someone got sick. There was never any time to play or go on picnics. Hospitals and nurses were everywhere. Relatives came to the house and talked only about sickness and doctors. The parent who was not sick was usually tired and depressed. One group member said, "Parents are more concerned about what the neighbors think than how the children are feeling."

The social worker said that it might be helpful to have a few parents come in and tell how it felt for them. The students decided to think about it for next time.

Karen and John left the room together. "Maybe we'll see each other around and talk some more," he said.

"I'd like that," she said as she waved good-bye.

Chapter 2

Does My Parent Have AIDS?

K aren wondered if anyone else in the group had a family member die from AIDS. When her father first got sick, she didn't know what kind of illness it was.

Most children in families with AIDS are not told directly about the illness, for two reasons. First, most people are not good at talking about any kind of illness. Second, AIDS has been known for only about twelve years, and many people are still afraid of it. Some parents do sit down with their children and talk about their illness. Some parents wait for the children to ask questions. In a few cases, children find out by hearing a doctor or parent talking about it.

There is only one way you can know for sure if your parent has AIDS: Ask directly and be told. AIDS looks like a lot of other diseases. People who have the disease often lose weight and are tired a lot, but losing weight and being tired can be caused by a hundred other problems.

If you think that your parent is ill and you want to talk to someone right away, turn to the "Help List" on page 60. Many numbers given there are free. Some places will tell you about support groups like the one that Karen and John attend. Most will not ask your name.

Most parents with AIDS have a hard time deciding whether or not to tell their children. Parents love their children and want their lives to be happy. They are afraid that other children who find out may make fun of their children and say mean things to them.

Parents—like children—sometimes have trouble admitting that they have problems. Adults may hope that things will get better or go away.

Karen's father went to work every day. He was a policeman and worked at the precinct near their apartment. His uniform didn't fit well because he was losing weight. He always had a reason why he was tired and why he didn't have time to eat. Her mother and father were fighting a lot, and Karen wondered if she was doing something wrong. She and her father used to go to the movies and for walks, but now he was always too tired.

It can take a while to get over the shock of learning that you have AIDS.

Karen's father had not been tested for HIV. He was afraid to find out the truth. How could he tell his wife and daughter if he was sick? How could he keep going, knowing that he had such a serious illness? He thought that it was better for no one else to know what was happening to him. Maybe all the symptoms he noticed were really nothing to worry about after all. He wanted to hold on to that thought.

Good people sometimes have bad things happen to them. And good people sometimes have a hard time admitting the truth.

What Does AIDS Look Like?

AIDS looks like the flu and many other illnesses. A person could have all the problems listed below and still *not* have AIDS. Here are some signs that an illness might be AIDS.

- weight loss
- fever
- frequent fatigue
- night sweats
- deep, persistent cough
- vision problems
- skin rashes and sores
- sores in the mouth
- diarrhea that doesn't go away.

Almost everyone has some of these symptoms some of the time. But a person with AIDS can't fight them off; they keep coming back.

How Is AIDS Treated?

Some doctors know a lot about AIDS because they have treated many patients. Doctors use drugs to help cure the sores and coughs and fevers. But at this time there is no cure for AIDS. Even though a person with AIDS can go to work and look healthy, sooner or later he or she will become very ill.

People with AIDS have good times when the drugs are working and the illness is resting. But they also have bad times when pneumonia or cancer or TB starts.

Some people take the drugs called AZT or DDI to help slow down the illness. For others, these drugs do more harm than good. Many people with AIDS try to help the body heal by paying attention to relaxation, diet, and exercise.

It is upsetting and scary for a parent with AIDS to feel good one day and bad the next. Your parent is losing control over his or her life . It is understandable that he or she often gets moody and angry at the doctor or at the other parent or at you. The parent doesn't want to hurt you. Feelings build up inside, and sometimes they come out at the wrong time or at the wrong person. Let your parent know if you are hurt. Both of you have a right to be hurt and angry. If your parent has AIDS, both your lives have changed. But knowing the facts about HIV and AIDS will help you and your parent to be stronger and healthier and to move on.

Chapter 3

Facts about HIV and AIDS

Karen didn't understand why some people used the term HIV and others said AIDS. She wondered whom to ask. She called one of the national hotlines in the "Help List" to find out. The person who answered was very nice, but when the call was over Karen still had questions. That day she called the hotline back five times because she wanted to understand all the facts. Knowing about the illness made her feel a little stronger and more in control. The workers at the hotlines will take as much time as you need and welcome your calling back as often as you like.

Some people use the terms HIV and AIDS as if they were the same. But that is wrong.

Since the disease AIDS has been known only about 12 years, some questions still cannot be answered. Two of the ways this disease is spread

There are many ways to gather information about AIDS.

are by drug use and sexual behavior. Therefore, it is often talked about only in whispers, and many myths are spread about it.

AIDS stands for *a*cquired *i*mmunodeficiency syndrome. The disease attacks the body's defense system. The body has many parts that work together to keep you healthy. If you get a cold or the flu, the defense system fights the germs and helps you get better. In a person with AIDS, that defense system doesn't work as well as it should. So when the person gets a cold or the flu, it is much harder for the body to fight the disease and recover.

The body's defense system also keeps you strong, so if you sit next to a person with a cold you usually won't catch it. The defense system prevents a lot of illness. When people with AIDS sit next to someone who is sick, they are likely to pick up the germs or infection. Their defense system is not working well.

HIV Causes AIDS

Most medical experts believe that AIDS is caused by a virus called HIV, which stands for *h*uman *i*mmunodeficiency *v*irus. Some doctors believe that HIV must be combined with other viruses to cause AIDS. HIV is a tiny live particle that enters the body through blood or sexual fluids. HIV can enter the body and not show up for many years. Or it can multiply and interfere with the body's workings.

Exposure to colds and flu can create serious problems for a person with AIDS.

Earvin "Magic" Johnson announces his retirement from the Los Angeles Lakers after testing positive for the AIDS virus.

HIV can grow silently in the body for 10 years or more. While it is in the body, it hurts the defense or protector cells that usually help keep people well. Once HIV is in the body, it does not go away.

A person with HIV is called "HIV-positive." He or she may look and act healthy for years. There is no way to know if someone is HIV-positive unless he or she has been tested and told you the results. The next chapter tells more about testing.

Being HIV-positive is not the same as having AIDS. A person can be healthy and have HIV. But sooner or later, a person with HIV will get AIDS. Having the disease AIDS means that the defense system has been damaged and the person has begun to contract some serious infections.

People with AIDS do not always look or act sick. Once the infections are treated, a person with AIDS can go to work and look normal. But after years of treatment, the body gets tired and has a hard time fighting off the infections.

Many doctors and scientists are working to find vaccines and cures, but no one knows how long it will take. The good news is that treatments are improving so that a person with AIDS can live a longer and healthier life.

Where Did HIV or AIDS Come From?

No one knows the answer to that question. In Canada and the United States, the first five cases of AIDS were reported in 1981. At first it was thought to be a disease of homosexuals and was called "gay-related immune deficiency." In 1982, it was renamed AIDS when doctors realized that anyone could contract it. It was not until 1983 that American and French doctors discovered that HIV was a cause of the illness.

AIDS is a worldwide problem. Doctors in every country are working to find better treatments and a cure. Africa and the United States have the most reported cases.

The next chapter discusses how you can protect yourself from AIDS. Right now that means protection from HIV.

Hugs are often the best medicine.

Chapter 4

Will I Get AIDS?

Karen was worried that she might get AIDS from her father. She didn't want to ask him. She began waking up in the middle of the night sweating and feeling scared. She wondered if she might be getting AIDS.

On a walk in the park with her father, Karen said that she needed to have a "heart to heart." That was what they called their private talks.

"I love you and don't want to stop hugging you, but I am having nightmares about getting AIDS. How can I be sure that I will never get it from you?" she asked.

Her father suggested that they go to the Department of Health AIDS information office and meet with a counselor. Even though he had read a lot

23

about AIDS, he wanted to make sure that all Karen's questions were answered with the most accurate and up-to-date facts.

"Let's take your mom and go down this afternoon," her father said.

The counselor at the office told them that getting AIDS from a relative just by living in the same household is extremely rare. HIV is never caught by everyday actions such as sharing dishes, toilets, and toothbrushes.

HIV can be spread by sharing infected drug needles, by having unprotected sex, or by passing it from a mother to an infant during pregnancy or childbirth. Before 1985, it could be spread in blood transfusions.

If someone with HIV lives in your household, it is wise to wear throwaway gloves if you change a bandage covering a deep cut or change a diaper. This will also protect you from other viruses, and it will protect the person from any infections you might be carrying. Since people with AIDS have a damaged defense system, they are more likely to catch something from you than you are from them.

If you find a drug needle in your home, do not touch it. Get an adult who will wear gloves and carefully dispose of the needle.

You cannot get HIV by hugging or kissing your parent. Hugs are very important to both of you. When you give and receive a hug, you are sharing love. Sometimes hugs are the best medicine.

Karen got pamphlets and a book from the counselor. She asked a few questions and listened very carefully.

The counselor said something odd at the end: "Even though you now know the facts, you might still be scared. If you keep having the fear of getting HIV from your father, it would be good to come to see a counselor for a few sessions.

"Fear does not always go away quickly. You have taken the best course of action. You have been honest about your feelings. And that means that people can help you. Keeping feelings secret only makes them worse. But sharing scary feelings is a way to understand and control them.

"I am very glad you came to see us today. Here is my telephone number. You can call any time with any question. No question is too silly. If you would like to call tomorrow to tell me how you are doing, that would be fine. You are a strong family who are sticking together at a tough time. I know that you will be able to help each other and also get help from others when you need it."

Karen now knew that she couldn't get HIV just by living in the same household with her father. But she wanted to know more about how to prevent ever getting AIDS from anyone. She was sure that many of her classmates knew very little about AIDS. She decided to do a presentation at school so she could teach herself and others how to avoid getting AIDS.

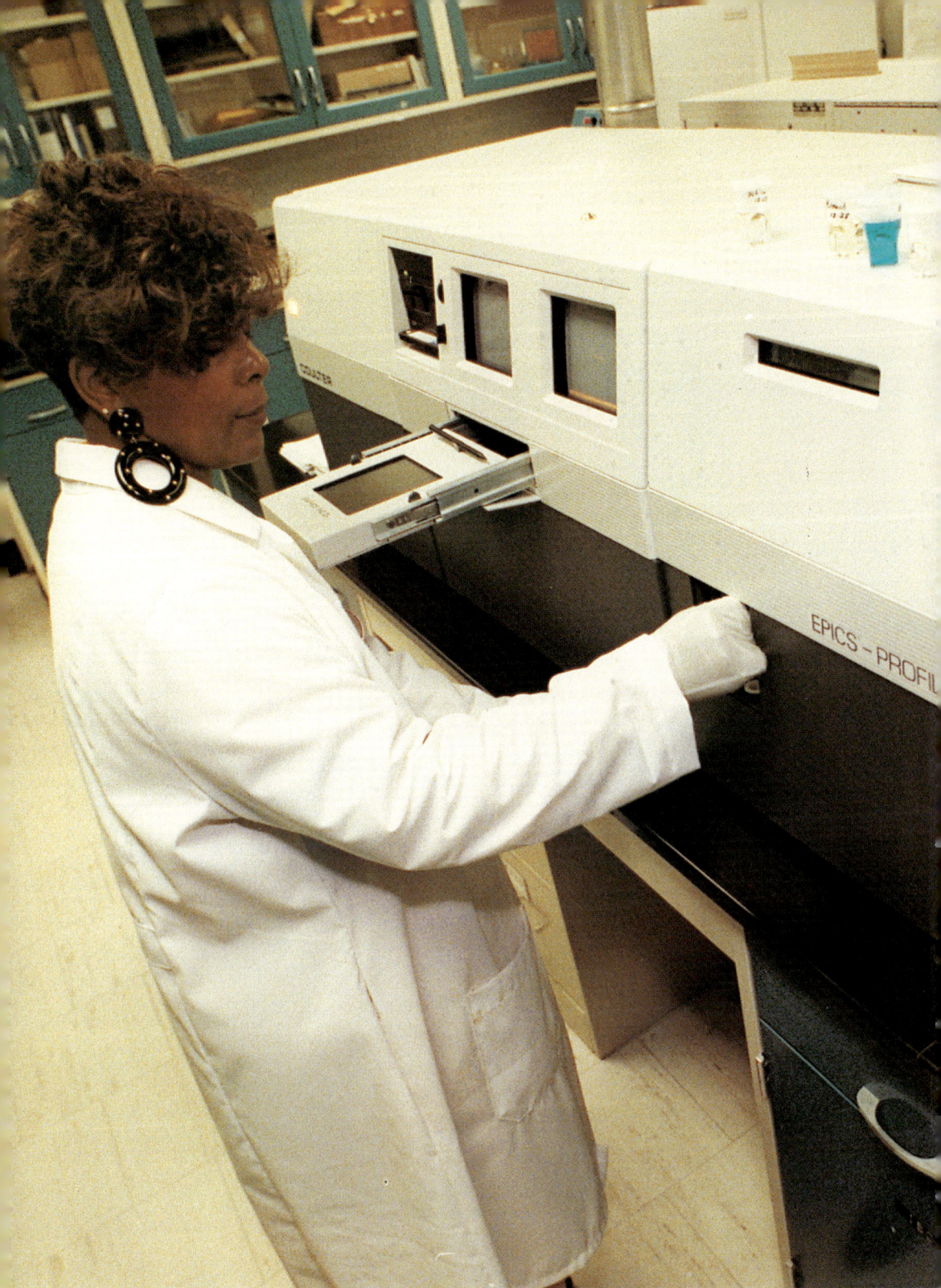

Blood is tested carefully for the presence of the HIV antibody.

Chapter 5

Preventing HIV

There are many rumors and myths about HIV. But the facts are quite simple. There are only *three* ways to get HIV.

Blood-to-blood contact

Some people use illegal drugs like heroin or steroids, which they inject into the body with a needle. If they share used needles, HIV-infected blood left in the needle can be passed to the next person using it. You should never use illegal drugs. However, people who do use drugs and needles should rinse the needle in bleach and water so that HIV-infected blood can never be passed to another person.

Before 1985, blood that people received in transfusions before an operation or to treat hemophilia was not tested. Sometimes it contained HIV. Since 1985, all blood is tested before it is used. Arthur Ashe, the famous tennis star, received a transfusion in the early 1980s and died in 1993 from AIDS. Most people who suffered from hemophilia before 1985 received HIV in transfusions. Ryan White, the young boy from the Midwest, contracted the HIV virus that way.

There is no risk in giving blood, because new needles are always used.

Sexual fluids to blood

During sexual activity, fluids from the body of one partner can come into contact with the blood of the other, usually through a sore or cut in the anus, vagina, penis, or mouth. HIV can pass from the fluids into the bloodstream. Saying no to sex is the only 100 percent safe way to avoid getting HIV sexually. As a young person, you will decide when and with whom you will have sex. This decision is a normal part of growing up. Talk about it with your parents, counselors, and friends. It doesn't matter what everyone else is doing. It matters what is best for you.

When you decide to have sex, have safer sex. That means being smart about preventing pregnancy and preventing HIV and other sexually transmitted diseases (STDs). Choose when to have a baby and choose never to have HIV. To prevent HIV, always use a new latex condom each time you have sexual intercourse.

Couples should be honest about their feelings and take responsibility for their actions.

Mother to fetus (child in the womb)

The baby of a woman with HIV will be born HIV-positive. During the first eighteen months of the baby's life, it may recover on its own. One out of three babies, however, remains HIV-positive and goes on to develop AIDS.

If you want to have a baby, consider being tested for HIV before having sex. Bringing a baby with HIV into the world will be very hard on you both. Parenthood is difficult enough. Parenthood with HIV is something you may want to avoid.

Ready for a quiz?

Which list of statements below is true? Which is false?

List A

HIV can rest quietly in the body for years.
No sex is the only 100 percent safe sex.
Teens can get HIV.
People with AIDS can work.
Some people don't know they have HIV.
Drug needles can be cleaned with bleach and water.
One parent can be HIV-positive, the other, HIV-negative.

List B

Only homosexuals get AIDS.
You can get HIV by lip kissing.
You can get AIDS from a mosquito bite.
You can get HIV in a swimming pool.
HIV and AIDS are the same thing.
There is no test for HIV.

List A is all true. List B is all false. The List B items are corrected below.

- Anyone can get AIDS—homosexuals, bisexuals, and heterosexuals. It is what you do, not who you are, that allows the virus to spread.
- Lip kissing does not put the sexual fluids in contact with blood.
- Mosquitoes do not transmit HIV from one person to another. Only drug needles, sex, or childbirth can do that.
- Swimming pools cannot contain HIV. HIV lives in blood or body fluids and dies in air or water.
- HIV is the virus that causes AIDS. Most people with the virus are well for a long time before getting AIDS.
- There is a test for HIV. You can find out where to be tested by calling your local health department or one of the numbers in the "Help List."

Now you know about HIV and AIDS. Help others learn the facts. Karen chose AIDS as a school project so she could learn more. You can bring up an AIDS question in your current events or health class. Everyone needs to know about HIV. Help spread the facts to others.

A parent with AIDS needs the loving support of his or her family.

Chapter 6

What AIDS Does to a Family

Karen wondered if her life would ever return to normal. Since her father got AIDS, it seemed that everything had changed. Even her grandmother, who had been the rock of the family, was upset. She blamed her son-in-law for getting the disease and was sure he would give it to her daughter. The Sunday trips to Grandma's were not as frequent and not as much fun.

John's mother had had cancer for three years. He knew what it was like to have his world turned upside down. He was bothered that his dad had been so secretive about Mom's illness. Was there any reason to be ashamed?

Sickness changes families, but not just for the worse. When families have major life crises such as sickness or death, both bad and good things happen. Shame, guilt, and stigma are some of the bad things. Pulling together and showing love are some of the good things.

Shame, Guilt, and Stigma

John's mother had cancer and his father treated it like a secret. John wondered why family members felt guilty about something over which they had no control. They never used the word cancer, as if pretending she didn't really have it.

Many adults have no idea how to handle a serious illness and death. They are overtaken, and they react, react, react. They run here, there, and everywhere without taking time to sit down and think about what is happening. It is often the first time in their lives that something has happened that can't be fixed.

Most problems have solutions. It may take time, work, money, or life changes, but most problems can be fixed. Serious diseases cannot always be controlled and sometimes can't be fixed. If adults have not dealt before with sickness and death, they are often thrown off balance.

Some families face the problem and go to their church or mental health worker or friends for help. But other families retreat and keep the secret.

No one deserves to be sick. No one wants to be sick. Whether it is AIDS or cancer or any other illness, the family did not do anything to deserve it.

Sometimes children think that they have done something to cause the illness. This is not true. When children can see the illness but are told nothing is wrong, they sometimes get confused and blame themselves. Children are not the cause of illness. If a child steals or lies, that does not cause illness. If a child does badly in school, skips school, or doesn't come home from school to be with the parent, it is not his or her fault if anything happens.

Bad things sometimes happen. Everyone wishes they didn't. But children can't cause someone to get sick, and they also can't make someone get better.

What Is Stigma?

Stigma means shame or dishonor or blot or stain. It means that someone tries to make you feel bad about something. If you are the only one in your class with a sick parent, some students may look at you funny. If you are the only black student in a white school, some people may make fun of you. Stigma is a bad feeling that someone sends your way because they think something is wrong with you.

There are two things you can do if people treat you badly. You can tell them that they are hurting you and ask them to stop. Or you can turn the other cheek and know that *they* have a problem—not you.

AIDS carries the most stigma of any disease. First, there are many myths about AIDS, and people are still afraid of getting it through casual contact. Second, it is carried by unsafe sex and drug use. Our society is not very good at talking about sex and drugs, so people do not want to talk about AIDS. Third, even though anyone can get AIDS from unsafe sex or drug use, certain groups of people have been hit hardest by the disease. To date, homosexual men and drug users have been hardest hit. Many people with AIDS are black or Hispanic. There is hate and prejudice against homosexuals, drug users, and people of color. Some people blame those with AIDS for having the disease.

Stigma and discrimination are ugly aspects of AIDS. People like Arthur Ashe, Ryan White, and Magic Johnson have all tried to make people think sensibly. Movie and music stars also have helped.

Many people are still afraid and are angry at people with AIDS. It is important for you to know that. The really bad part about stigma is believing that the person who treats you badly is right. If people don't like you because someone in your family has HIV, that is mostly their problem. But if you agree with them and start not liking yourself, the problem is yours, too.

People who are sick don't need blame. They need help. No one deserves AIDS or any other illness. Illness is not a punishment.

It is important for everyone to learn about illness and death and how to deal with them because they will happen to us all. It is also vital to learn about AIDS so we can prevent it and help others who have the disease.

Pulling Together and Showing Love

A good thing about illness and hardship is that they can bring people together. Family members often take one another for granted. They act as if everything will always stay the same. But life takes many unexpected turns. These turns cause us to realize what we have and appreciate it more. AIDS has brought many families together. It has given them a chance to express their love for one another. Many families with AIDS have gotten help from friends, neighbors, churches, and social service agencies.

When bad things happen, some families fall apart for a while. But most families recover and begin to pull together in a new and loving way. Many people stop taking drugs when they are diagnosed with AIDS. They want to take better care of themselves. They have a new desire to live free of drugs and enjoy their loved ones. AIDS is not all bad. Often good things happen. When people pull together and focus their lives on love, faith, and support, it feels good. Some of the things that once seemed important no longer matter so much.

A caring friend will be glad to listen to your problems.

Chapter 7

Whom Can I Tell?

Karen's dad had been very open with his family when he was diagnosed with AIDS. He sat down with his wife and daughter and said, "I am very sad to tell you that my doctor thinks I have AIDS. The test results are not back yet, but the doctor is quite sure that my pneumonia is a special kind called PCP."

Her father found out in 10 days that his illness was AIDS. He sobbed and apologized to his wife and daughter. "I am so sorry to put you through all this. You don't deserve it. I don't know what to do about work and which of my friends to tell. I can't even guess who will give me a hug and who will turn away. I have heard stories about people losing their apartments and jobs once others know that they have AIDS. We have to protect ourselves."

Karen was dazed. This was the worst day of her life. Her father had AIDS. No one knew if her mother was infected. Her father asked that the family not talk about the illness to anyone.

"I don't think I can handle all this," Karen said. "Is it okay if I talk to Marlena about it? She is my best friend, and I know that her older sister died of AIDS—even though I promised never to tell that I knew."

Her father agreed that she should talk to Marlena. "Everyone needs a best friend to share secrets with," he said. "We have to protect ourselves, but we can't become liars to all the people we love."

Making Promises

When people first learn of an HIV or AIDS diagnosis, they often promise themselves that they will never tell anyone. But living with a secret is very hard to do and very stressful. If the secret has to do with health, many medical people need to know. There is no right or wrong about whom to tell or when. But try not to make promises, because they are hard to keep.

Family

Parents have a hard time deciding whether to tell their children, their parents, or their friends. It isn't simple. Sometimes parents tell their older children, but not the younger ones. Sometimes a

Many families dealing with AIDS find it helpful to talk to a counselor.

baby in the family is HIV-positive, and the parents don't know whether to tell the other children.

It is good to talk about secrets and AIDS with your parents. Some families keep the news within the family. Some tell only close relatives and best friends. A few families become media teachers and tell their story on television or in classrooms. They hope they can lessen the fear and stigma for all.

Before telling others about HIV in your family, think back to other secrets you have shared and make a guess about who will stick by you.

Counselors

Counselors are trained to help people like you talk about problems. Counselors may be psychiatrists, social workers, or psychologists. They know how to be good listeners, which is not easy. Counselors don't usually tell you what to do. They help you figure out what to do.

Counselors never tell anyone what you say except in two cases. If you tell a counselor that you are being abused, he or she will report the fact to others who will protect you. If you tell a counselor that you plan to harm yourself or someone else, that also will be reported to others.

Many families with AIDS find it helpful to talk to a counselor. Some counselors' services are free. Some are paid for by your health insurance. And some are expensive. Try to find one that you can afford whose office is close to your home.

Welfare and Other Benefits

The federal, state, and local governments provide money and services to people who are sick and needy. These programs help with rent, or with hospital costs, or to buy food.

Your parent will choose whether or not to tell the social worker about AIDS in your family. Deciding whom to tell has to do with what good things you may get or what bad things might come of your telling. Can you get all the same services without telling? Are there special services available for people with AIDS?

Times of crisis give you new information about your friends. And times of crisis offer a chance to meet new friends who share similar problems.

Karen was happy to be part of the support group at school. She and John were becoming best friends. They understood each other in ways no one else could.

The time might come when a parent with AIDS needs to go to the hospital.

Chapter 8

What Illness and Death Look Like

Karen had never known anyone who was sick except for a cold or the flu. It scared her to wake up and hear her father coughing in a way that made his whole body shake. Twice her mother had to call an ambulance in the night, and Karen awoke to the blare of the siren.

Going to the hospital was also scary. People in white jackets were always racing through the halls, and Karen felt lost. Visiting hours were at the wrong time for her, and there were other patients in the room. She wanted some private time with her father, but he was too sick to get up and go to the lounge.

There are no perfect things to say to someone who is ill. But you do not have to figure out what to do. You can ask:

- Is there something I can get for you?
- Would you like to rest or sleep for a while?
- Am I talking too much?
- How long would you like me to stay?

People in the hospital need to be able to make choices.

It is a good idea to take a book or magazine for yourself when visiting. If your parent is very sick, just having you nearby will help.

Some parents and children decide not to have visits while in the hospital. That is okay. Each family needs to work out the best way for them.

John always felt as if he said the wrong thing when he visited his mother. He hated the hospital. He loved her, but whatever he said seemed to come out wrong.

No one knows the perfect way to behave when visiting someone who is ill. Here are a few hints:

- Share how you are feeling with your parent. Laughing, crying, and being scared are all okay.
- Ask about the illness if there are things you want to know.
- Try to keep any promises you make about visiting. It is lonely in a hospital, and your parent will be waiting to see you.
- Express your love. It is always the right time to tell a parent how much you care.

Visiting a sick parent in the hospital may be difficult, but it will often comfort both you and the patient.

Coma and Dementia

A coma is a condition of deep sleep in which the patient does not eat or speak or respond. Doctors are not sure whether a person in a coma can hear or feel. Some people go into a coma before they die. Others go into a coma for hours or days or weeks and then wake up.

It is hard to know whether to visit and what to do if your parent is in a coma. Some family members continue visiting; others stop for a while.

Dementia is a condition of confusion. It can be caused by the disease or by strong drugs. People with dementia act strangely and often don't make sense in what they say or do. They may stop recognizing their family or mix up family members.

Dementia is sometimes the last stage of the illness. This can be very upsetting to family members. Just make sure that you express yourself. Say how you feel no matter how demented the parent is. No one knows how much people who are at death's door really understand.

Anger and Sadness

It is normal to feel angry that someone you love is sick. Why is it your parent? Why is it AIDS? Why can't you go out and play like everyone else? Why can't anyone fix it? These are all good questions that have no good answers.

Sadness is an emotion that everyone feels. It often comes after a loss. You can lose a possession or a friend or a teacher. With AIDS, you can lose a parent or sibling to death. It is better to let the sadness out than hold it in. At one time, men never wanted anyone to see them cry. Now they are starting to admit it when they feel sad.

If your anger and sadness never seem to go away, you can arrange to see a counselor who can help you deal with it. If anger and sadness build up, exercising and taking time for yourself are two good ways for you to relax and get your energy back. Try to make time each day to do things that you enjoy.

You may even forget about your own health. Pay attention to what you eat. Remember to exercise. And don't be surprised if you need a little more sleep.

After a Parent Dies

Losing someone you love is very painful and confusing. How do you know when someone is dead? What happens after death? What happens to the spirit?

These are hard questions to answer. Doctors decide when someone is dead. With medical changes and new machines, death has a changing definition. Presently, doctors measure brain activity and breathing.

Religions have different ideas about death and an afterlife. Also, each person has his or her own beliefs.

It is important to allow yourself to grieve for a parent who has died.

Funerals

Funerals are usually religious services to mark the end of life on earth. At some funerals the minister, priest, or rabbi and some family members and friends talk about the loved one.

Funerals are usually held two to six days after the death. Families who know that their parent is very ill can plan the funeral ahead of time. Thinking about a funeral or planning it will not make it happen sooner. It will give the family time to make some of the hard choices.

Some people choose to bury the body at a cemetery; others choose to have the body cremated into ashes. Often this decision has been made earlier by the ill person.

If the body is to be buried, at the end of the funeral it is taken to a burial ground and a prayer is said before the body is lowered into the ground.

If the body has been cremated, the ashes are sometimes kept by the family in an urn or scattered at a favorite place such as a lake or mountain or garden.

In big families, there are often lots of people around the house to help during the week after a death. Some children feel their home has been invaded. Others find this helpful because there are people to talk to and play with. Take a moment when the time seems right to tell your other parent or someone close to you how you feel. Your needs are important, too.

Focusing on good memories will help to ease the pain of losing a parent.

Chapter 9

Starting Again

If your parent dies, you may wonder if your life will ever feel "normal" again. The answer is yes. Grief and mourning take a different length of time for each person, but they will end. Getting on with your life does not mean forgetting your parent. In fact, you always carry the memories of your times together.

At some time in the mourning process, you will begin to turn your eyes from the past toward the future. But mourning takes its twists and turns.

Karen said that mourning was like an ocean wave. One day the memory of her father felt like a cool wave on a hot day. The next day the wave would knock her off her feet when she didn't even see it coming. She could never guess whether

seeing someone who looked like him would make
her smile or cry. It always made her feel out of
control.

After a while, she began to plan her own future.
What would her father have wanted for her? What
did she want for herself? College was the answer
to both questions, so she began to study hard and
face the future with boldness.

Karen thought about the support group she
would attend today. This was her sixth session,
and she was now much more relaxed when she
came into the room. The social worker began:

"Today we're going to talk about how you are
dealing with your new household. What is it like
for those of you with new guardians? What is it like
for those of you with only one parent? I'm sure it is
very different for each of you."

Richard talked about how he had moved to his
grandmother's apartment after his mother died.
He hadn't seen his father since babyhood. His
grandmother had changed now that she was the
"Parent." She had old ideas about curfew and
hanging out that Richard found hard to obey. But
he also knew that it was hard for her. She was
sixty-five years old and had taken Richard and his
younger sisters into her small apartment. Some
days her knees were so sore that she needed help
getting out of bed.

John and his father got along pretty well except
for one thing: when his father went out to dinner

with a woman. John was not ready to have another mother, and he resented the time that his father took to be with anyone else. John wanted it to be just his father and him.

One day after John had been rude to a friend of his dad's, they had a long talk. John said he understood his dad's wanting a girlfriend, but it was too soon. Every time he saw his dad with another woman, he felt like throwing up. He couldn't explain exactly how he felt. John's father agreed not to bring women to their house for a while. He would continue to date and would tell John where he was going. But John felt better because it wasn't "in his face." They both agreed to try this arrangement for a while and have another talk in a few months.

Karen talked about how sad and depressed her mother was. She wished that she would start being social—with anyone. Karen felt guilty about going out and leaving her at home. She talked to her mother about seeing a counselor, but her mother was too sad to reach out for help. Karen was worried and arranged a private meeting with the social worker to talk about her mother.

Everyone in the group agreed that there were up days and down days. Going back to school, making new friends, setting up new routines, and getting used to a new household all helped. Talking about feelings and knowing that you weren't the only one having them also helped.

Getting involved with good friends in positive activities will make the future seem bright again.

Wishes and Dreams

Life has many ups and downs. The loss of a parent is often one of the biggest downs. It is very hard to lose a parent when you are a teen.

As a young person, you may have 50, 60, or 70 years ahead of you. Parents who know they are going to die regret that they will not get to see their children grow up, perhaps raise a family of their own, and be successful. All parents dream of a wonderful future for their children.

You have a chance to have that wonderful future. Think about where you would like to be in 10 years, and make a plan to get there. Do not worry about changing your mind. You can change your plan as often as you change your mind.

Some people think that being rich or successful comes from making all the right choices. But famous people will usually tell you they got that way by hard work, a lucky break, and lots of mistakes. Don't be afraid to make mistakes; they teach you how to make better choices in the future.

Successful people also accept what happens and start again. If they suffer a knockdown blow, they get up, brush themselves off, and start again with dreams for a better tomorrow.

You have survived one of life's hardest blows—the loss of a parent. Go forward with your dreams. You deserve good things. With hard work, a lucky break, and lots of mistakes, you can get there, too.

Glossary—*Explaining New Words*

AZT Drug that slows down the HIV virus.

bisexual Person who has sex with both males and females.

coma Condition of unconsciousness caused by disease or injury.

condom Thin latex sheath placed on the penis before sex.

counseling Discussing problems with a trained person.

dementia Impairment of reasoning ability and mental awareness, usually caused by brain damage.

drug Substance taken into the body to change the mood or feeling.

gay A man who prefers a man as his sexual and life partner, or a woman who prefers a woman as her partner.

hemophilia Hereditary disease of males that affects the clotting of the blood.

heterosexual Preferring a sexual and life partner of the opposite sex.

homosexual Preferring a sexual and life partner of the same sex.

immune system System in the body that fights infection and disease.

injecting drug user Person who uses drugs through a hypodermic needle.

sexual intercourse Sexual activity in which the penis is placed inside the vagina or rectum of a partner.

stigma Imagined mark of disgrace placed on a person because of perceived differences in appearance or behavior.

transfusion Blood given after or during an operation.

transmission Passage of a virus or germ from one person to another.

virus Cell that takes over another cell. Viruses besides HIV are polio, herpes, and the common cold.

Help List

In Your Community
Often it is people near your home who know the best places to call. Teachers and counselors have up-to-date information. Your family doctor or church or temple are also good places to start.

Hotlines
You don't have to give your name when you call any of the numbers below. You might be asked where you are from or your age, nothing else.
All numbers beginning with 1-800 are FREE to the caller.

In the United States
National AIDS Hotline (English)
1-800-342-AIDS or 342-2437

National AIDS Hotline SIDA (Spanish)
1-800-344-SIDA or 344-7432

National AIDS Hotline TTY (Hearing Impaired)
1-800-AIDS-TTY or 243-7889

National Institute of Drug Abuse
1-800-662-HELP

Hemophilia Foundation
1-212-682-5510 (you may call collect)

National AIDS Clearinghouse
P.O. Box 6003
Rockville, MD 20850

National Pediatric HIV Center
1-800-362-0071

National Sexually Transmitted Disease Hotline
1-800-234-TEEN or 234-8336

In Canada
Toronto: AIDS Hotline
1-416-340-8844 (you may call collect)

Montreal: AIDS Committee
1-514-282-9991 (you may call collect)

Vancouver: PWA Vancouver
1-604-893-2250

For Further Reading

Bell, Ruth. *Changing Bodies, Changing Lives: A Book for Teens on Sex and Relationships.* New York: Random House Vintage Books, 1988.

Hein, Karen, M.D. *AIDS: Trading Fears for Facts.* New York: Consumers Union, 1989.

Johnson, Earvin "Magic." *What You Can Do to Avoid AIDS.* New York: Times Books, 1992.

Krementz, Jill. *How It Feels When a Parent Dies.* New York: Alfred A. Knopf, 1992.

Madaras, Lynda. *Lynda Madaras Talks to Teens about AIDS.* New York: Newmarket Press, 1988.

Shire, Amy. *Everything You Need to Know When You Are HIV-Positive.* New York: Rosen Publishing Group, 1994.

Taylor, Barbara, rev. ed. *Everything You Need to Know about AIDS.* New York: Rosen Publishing Group, 1992.

Weiner, L., Best, A., and Pizzo, P. *Be a Friend: Children with HIV Speak.* Morton Grove, IL: Whittman and Co., 1994.

Index

AIDS
    fear of, 23, 25, 42
    how it is (and is not) spread,
      24, 27–28, 30
    questions about, 12
    symptoms of, 12, 14
    telling others about, 12, 14,
      39–40, 42–43
    testing for, 14, 30, 31
    treatment for, 15, 21
anger, 48–49
Ashe, Arthur, 28, 36

Blood-to-blood contact (and
    AIDS) 24, 27–28

Coma, 48
condoms, 28
counselor, 23–25, 42, 49, 55
cure, finding for AIDS, 21

Death, 45–46, 48–49, 51, 57
dementia, 48
drug use (and AIDS), 18, 24, 27,
    31

Family (how AIDS affects),
    33–37
funerals, 51

Government assistance, 43
grieving, 53

Help, getting, 37
hemophilia, 27
HIV, 15
    contracting, 27–28, 30–31
    facts about, 16, 24
    how it causes AIDS, 18,
      20–21
homosexuality (and AIDS), 21,
    30, 31, 36
hospital
    going to, 45
    visiting, 46
hugging (and AIDS), 24

Johnson, Magic, 36

Kissing (and AIDS), 24, 30,
    31

Preventing infection, 24–25, 27–28

Religion, role of, 49, 51

Safe sex, 28
shame (and AIDS), 33, 37, 42
sexual behavior (and AIDS) 18,
     24, 28, 31
social worker, 7, 8, 9, 10, 42, 43

stigma, 35–36 (*see also* shame)
support group, 12, 43, 54, 55

Vaccine, creating, 21

Welfare, 43
White, Ryan, 28, 36
what to say (to someone who is
     ill), 46

About the Author
Barbara Draimin is a social work administrator for the
Division of AIDS Services in New York City. She designs
and implements programs for children and their families
who have AIDS. The Division serves over 2,500 families.
     Ms. Draimin holds a Doctorate of Social Welfare from
the City University of New York and Master's degrees from
the Hunter College School of Social Work and Boston
University School of Education.

Photo Credits
Cover photo by Stuart Rabinowitz.
Pages 2, 6, 13, 17, 19, 22, 29, 32, 44, 47, 50, 52, 56: Stuart
Rabinowitz; pages 20, 26: Wide World Photos, Inc.; page 38:
Mary Lauzon.

Design/Production Blackbirch Graphics, Inc.